W9-DCF-785

Date Due

BC 1 '81			
DEC 8 1981			
BC 3 82			
Feb 12			
KTR Mar 83			
JAN 25			

QUEBEC AND THE ST LAWRENCE

QUEBEC AND THE ST LAWRENCE

Photographs by John de Visser and Paul von Baich

Introduction by Yves Thériault

Toronto
OXFORD UNIVERSITY PRESS
1980

The following photographs in this book are by Paul von Baich:
Plates 10, 12, 19, 20, 28, 30, 32, 33, 35, 40, 41, 43, 46, 48a, 48b, 49, 71.
The jacket image and all other photographs are by John de Visser.

Designed by FORTUNATO AGLIALORO

©Oxford University Press (Canadian Branch) 1980
ISBN 0-19-540337-1
1 2 3 4 – 3 2 1 0
Printed in Hong Kong by
EVERBEST PRINTING COMPANY LIMITED

INTRODUCTION
by Yves Thériault

Here is the whole length of a noble river, its shorelines, isles, and promontories—nearly 1,200 splendid miles, one rarely like another, always enticing, and a constant source of astonishment and joy. This book portrays the St Lawrence on its majestic way with something also of the towns it passes—cities of commerce like Montreal, places of industry like Sorel, of confluence like Trois-Rivières, of comfortable serenity like Rimouski, of haunting memory like Quebec.

The St Lawrence issues from Lake Ontario and in this book we begin our journey at Kingston, but for most of its course the river is Québécois and proud of that fact. To appreciate this to the full one must see it flowing so calmly below its own city of Quebec. 'It's fine!' say my countrymen. 'Oh it's fine!' You don't see a town like that by waters such as these without breathing a sigh of pleasure.

The St Lawrence lingers at Montreal, having lost a good few hours teasing its way twice through a thousand islands—first among the famous international ones up near Kingston, and then among the not-so-well-known ones behind Montreal, around Laval. These are the other thousand islands, cousins of the first group and also pretty, but often forgotten—poor cousins that aren't even mentioned anymore on the big maps. The St Lawrence, having arrived among them, struggles against the force of the Ottawa River, holding it back just long enough to girdle the Ile Perrot, and then swirls on beyond Laval into yet another archipelago. One family of islands is followed by another and yet another: the islands of Boucherville, then those at Sorel, and all the others lower down. The St Lawrence is full of islands, as is the gulf; and the North Shore is liberally sprinkled with them. It is as though the river were enamoured of their shores.

What airs and graces the St Lawrence puts on at Quebec, as it rises and falls with the tide at Cap Diamant! On the crest of the hill is the Château Frontenac, a mere hotel become a castle by virtue of its bearing, position, and geography. Fortified and garrisoned, it could command the entire extent of these waters. No warship could prevail against the slopes on which it stands.

So here we are at Quebec, where breathes the history of New France. Narrow, winding streets; old horse-drawn carriages; proud, lofty monuments; a ruling Parliament; and, on the other shoulder of the hill, the bourgeois town—a little mannered, a little run-down, looking from its back door at a valley whose slopes rise towards the gentle peaks of the Laurentians and a broad, wild forest, full of game, that seems on a clear day so near as to be within call. In this Quebec, where ancient, historic houses are neighbours to the most blatant modernism, we find the Quebeckers, hospitable, obliging, open and honest, old-fashioned in their manners and habits, looking down from a slightly antique viewpoint on other towns that may be smaller but are much more developed. Quebec attracts and casts its spell by promises of a tempo and a rhythm from the past: among old, stone buildings one almost expects ancient courtiers to appear, faithful subjects of the King of France, ready to defend their colony against the 'savages' and to fill the holds of their ships with pelts bartered for glass beads in the villages of friendly tribes.

Where else in North America can one find such contrasts: between the old town and the new; between the upper town and the lower; between the forest nearby and skyscrapers of glass and concrete, which in turn exist side by side with ancient dwellings and the remains of fortifications; or between ancient alleyways and boulevards so wide as to seem like rivers of asphalt? Quebec is a city that stirs the soul: noble, dramatic, and gracious as the river beside which it stands.

The St Lawrence, remarkable in its narrows, is no less so when it embraces the horizon. Think of its banks and its islands, of how — seemingly tired of steep, overpowering heights — it relaxes gently on long, low beaches, sometimes of sand, sometimes of black rocks, as at Gros Morne. As soon as its waters lap the North Shore it plays like a cat, twisting and curling along the winding coastlines, reefs and cliffs, round islands and long flat slabs of basalt. Held back by a group of seven islands, the river forms a harbour, which once gave shelter to the whole fleet of a great naval power. Then it flows on towards the incomparable reaches of the Lower North Shore, a coast that is wild and sand-strewn as far as the eye can see, throwing out more islands, falling back in deep coves cut by the tide, raising up granite headlands against the heavy green waters.

While restlessly beating against the changing shores of the left bank, the river spreads out on the right to form a gulf and pretends to the limitless dimensions of a sea. The Magdalen Islands, hidden in shrouds of mist on the edge of the curving horizon, at last come faintly into view. Out in the open heart of its expanse the river bears up the great green ship of Anticosti Island — surging along its flanks, then becoming suddenly quieted, calm and disciplined, as though concerned not to disturb this sleeping giant. On warm autumn days, when the sun hangs heavy, languid vapours rise from water caught between the rocks to mingle with some cumulus or cirrus cloud that draws them upward into the deep blue sky.

And so the river-gulf slips away.

The waters of this unique river, balanced by the tides, are inexhaustibly rich in colour and texture, never foul or gloomy — a powerful, easy flood, a constant surge that rises far away inland, wanders lightly, tumbles here, overflows there, touches, caresses, and without the slightest hesitation scorns all impediments and finally merges with the ocean somewhere out on the edge of the Atlantic between the Labrador Peninsula and Newfoundland.

Vistas and structures, night and brilliant sun, the colours made by man and those given to nature by God — these things offer a new enchantment on every page of this book. However excellent the pictures are, they only hint to the stranger and the stay-at-home that a thousand more marvels are waiting there to be found. A feast for the eye, this, but only a window after all that one wants to open so as to see more beyond....

Translated by Roger Boulton

LIST OF PLATES

1

2

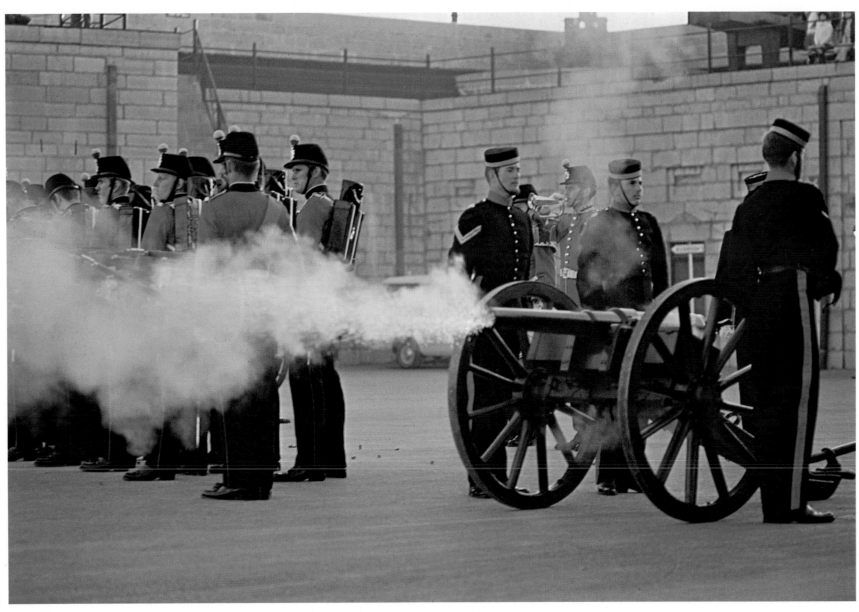

3

4

5

12

13

20

21

22

23

6 27

a   b

29

33

36

37

45

48 a

48 b

4

56

57

60

61

64   65

70 71

86

87

88